READING

Vikings

Stewart Ross

Aladdin/Watts
London • Sydney

Contents

This edition published in 2003

© Aladdin Books Ltd 2000

Designed and produced by
Aladdin Books Ltd
28 Percy Street
London W1T 2BZ

First published in
Great Britain in 2000 by
Franklin Watts
96 Leonard Street
London EC2A 4XD

ISBN 0 7496 5082 6

All rights reserved

Printed in U.A.E.

Editor: Jim Pipe

Historical Consultant
Antony Mason

Series Literacy Consultant
Wendy Cobb

Design
Flick, Book Design and Graphics

Picture Research
Brooks Krikler Research

A catalogue record for this book is
available from the British Library.

Viking Attack!

The priest looked out at the ships sailing from the north. He called to his friends. They had never seen strange ships like these. Who did they belong to?

When the ships landed, big men with fair hair jumped ashore. They carried swords and axes. Soon they were running towards the buildings where the priests lived.

The strangers must have been very scary!

The raiders looked for treasure.

A few priests went to welcome the strangers. But the strangers did not want to talk. They killed the priests and ran on. The other priests shut the gates and windows, and started praying.

The raiders smashed down the gates. They killed the priests and stole everything they could find.

Priests often kept holy treasures.

This attack happened about 1,200 years ago. The priests lived on an island off the coast of northern England, called Lindisfarne.

The first raiders sailed from Norway, a land in north-west Europe. Later, other raiders came from the nearby lands of Sweden and Denmark.

They attacked England and many other lands in southern and western Europe, such as Ireland, Germany, France and Spain.

The English called the raiders "Northmen". The French knew them as "Normans".

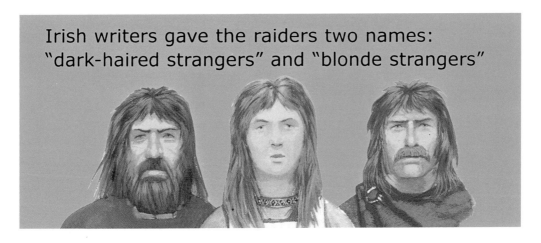

Irish writers gave the raiders two names: "dark-haired strangers" and "blonde strangers"

Later, writers living in Iceland called the raiders "Vikings". This name was soon very popular. Nowadays, everyone knows the fierce raiders from Norway, Sweden and Denmark as Vikings.

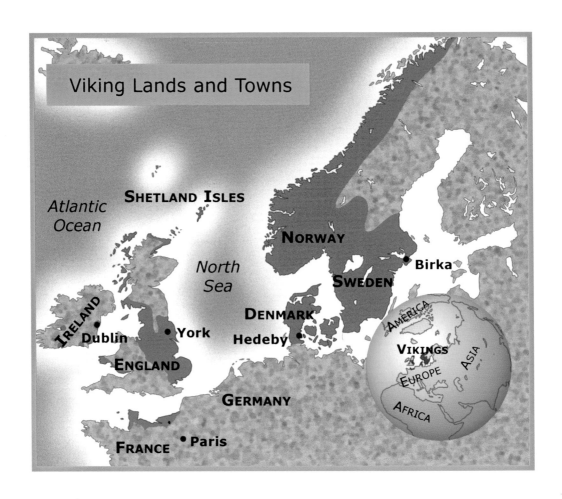

The Vikings raided Europe for 300 years. But they weren't just warriors. Most were farmers or traders. Some were great artists and poets.

They also sailed across the Atlantic Ocean to North America. If you want to find out more about their adventures, then read on!

Sea Raiders

The Vikings were brave and fought fiercely with big axes. They were also very good sailors. No one knew where they would attack next, so it was very difficult to fight back.

The Viking raiders sailed up rivers or left their ships on beaches. They stole horses and made surprise attacks on farms, villages, towns and holy places.

Viking warriors had bows and arrows. But they preferred to fight with swords, axes and spears.

Only the most important Vikings wore armour.

Viking ships had very flat bottoms. So the Vikings could row up even shallow rivers.

Before any large army could fight them, the Vikings ran back to their ships and sailed away. For more than 300 years, the people of north-west Europe lived in terror.

Vikings from Norway raided Scotland and Ireland, then went south to France. Vikings from Denmark, known as the Danes, attacked

England, France and Spain. Vikings from Sweden sailed to the Black Sea (map on page 17).

The first Viking raiders went west in the summer, when the weather was warm and the sea was calm. They sailed in a few ships and went home before the autumn storms.

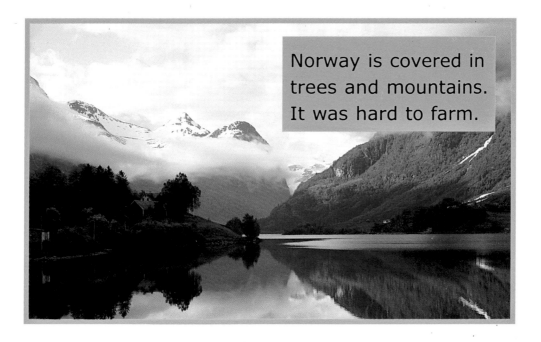

Norway is covered in trees and mountains. It was hard to farm.

Back in the Viking lands, life was tough. In winter, the ground was covered in snow. The land was hard to farm. Families were often hungry because there wasn't enough food.

When warriors told their friends and families about the rich farms and towns they had seen, more Vikings went raiding.

Viking ships could carry an army up most rivers.

In time, fleets of ships carried Viking armies to the south. The armies did not come to burn and rob. They came to win new lands.

Women and children went with them too. They built houses and settled down in the lands the warriors had won.

The Vikings settled in England, Ireland and northern France. They built new towns like Dublin in Ireland and York in England.

One Viking king, Canute (say "ca-newt"), ruled over England, Norway, Denmark and Sweden.

Viking armies also attacked big towns like Paris, in France.

Explorers & Traders

Greenland and America • Longboats • Russia

The Vikings were not just warriors. They were also explorers and traders.

Once, some Vikings got lost in the Atlantic Ocean. They saw a large island covered in ice and snow and called it "Ice Land" (Iceland). Ten years later, other Vikings came to live there.

A Viking town in Greenland

Writers gave nicknames to some famous Vikings . Erik the Red had red hair, but some people think he was also called "red" because he often got angry.

Erik the Red was a famous Viking from Iceland. He sailed west and found another new land. He called it "Green Land" (Greenland). This made it sound greener than it really was!

Leif, Erik the Red's son, sailed even further west. We are not sure exactly where he went, but he did reach Canada.

This was the first time people from Europe had come to North America. They called it "Vine Land" because grape vines grew there.

Vikings in North America traded with the local people.

People still make boats using Viking tools and methods.

The Vikings built wonderful boats. They were fast and strong and could sail through the roughest seas.

Warriors used long, narrow boats called "longboats". The boats were light enough to carry over land between rivers. Many had dragon shapes carved at the front.

On the open sea, longboats used their sails. Near the shore and on rivers, the warriors rowed with long oars.

Traders used a type of boat called a "knorr" (say "nor"). It was wider than a longboat, so there was room for goods. Some knorrs may have had a deck to keep the goods dry.

A big storm could sink a Viking boat.

Voyages were cold and wet. People wrapped up in animal furs to keep warm. They ate dried food and drank water from leather bottles.

The Viking port of Hedeby (see map on page 6) was a big centre for trade. What goods can you see in this picture?
Answer on page 32.

The Vikings did not have maps. They tried to stay near the shore so they knew where they were. Away from land, they found their way by watching the sun, moon and stars.

Viking traders travelled all over Europe by boat, horse, cart and even sledge. They took with them furs and goods made of iron and bone. They traded these for gold, silver, silks and spices.

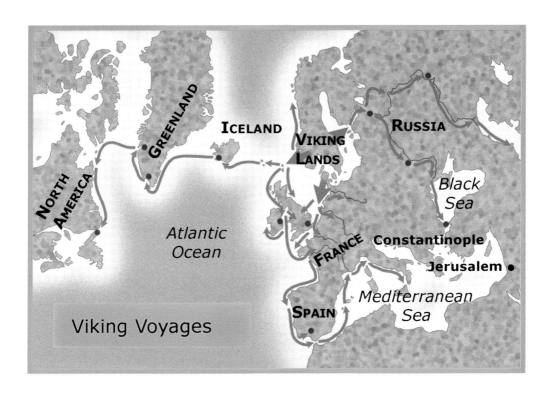

Viking Voyages

The traders set up bases in Russia. A few went even further and reached the ancient city of Jerusalem (now in Israel).

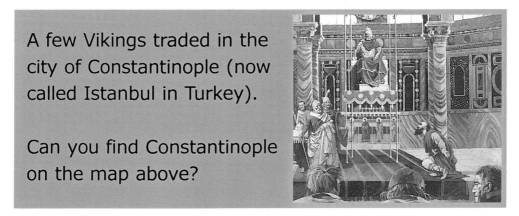

A few Vikings traded in the city of Constantinople (now called Istanbul in Turkey).

Can you find Constantinople on the map above?

Farms & Towns

Food • Homes • Crafts • Clothes

Most Vikings did not go on raids or explore far-off lands. They were country people. They got up at sunrise and went early to bed.

They spent their days farming, fishing, hunting or doing housework. When they went to live in a new land, they took their way of life with them.

Some brave Vikings hunted whales for food.

What are these Viking foods?
Hint: **a** is a big animal.
Answers on page 32.

Viking farmers grew oats, barley and vegetables. They also grew fruit, such as apples and nuts. These were stored for the winter. They fished and also hunted for seals, bears, deer, rabbits and foxes.

Most Viking houses were made of wood. Some walls were made by sticking clay (called daub) onto a screen of twigs (called wattle).

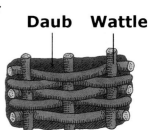

Daub   Wattle

The roofs were covered with straw or turf. In places where there weren't any trees, houses were made of stone or earth.

Most houses had just one large, long room. The windows were holes in the wall. In cold weather and at night they blocked up the windows with boards.

Women cooked on an open fire in the middle of the floor. This kept the house warm too. The smoke went out through a hole in the roof.

In the winter, families shared homes with their animals. It must have been very smoky and smelly inside.

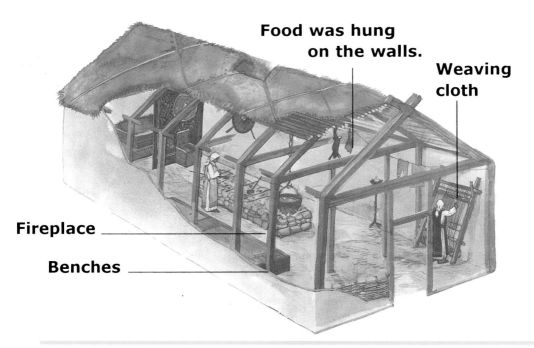

Food was hung on the walls.

Weaving cloth

Fireplace

Benches

This woman is wearing Viking clothes. Can you see what she's doing? (Answer on page 32.)

Viking women ran the house, doing the cooking and looking after the children. The children did not go to school. They helped in the house or out in the fields.

At night the Vikings lit their houses with fish oil lamps. The lamps were stuck to a long pole which was pushed into the ground.

The Vikings had little furniture. But they were very skilful at carving wood for special items.

Front of a ship

Bucket

Cradle

Sledge

Each Viking family, or group of families, made
their own clothes.
The women sewed
them from wool or
linen cloth.

Most Vikings took great care over their looks.
They liked bright colours, long dresses, swirling
cloaks and heavy jewellery. Both Viking men
and women may have worn eye make-up.

The Vikings used
sledges to cross the
snow, like people do
today. But horses
pulled their sledges.
The Vikings also used
skis and ice skates.

Bone skates

Rules & Gods

Vikings had to obey the law. Once a year, each town held a meeting, called a "thing", to sort out arguments or vote for a new chief.

If someone killed another Viking, they had to pay money to the family of the person they had killed. But thieves were hanged.

The most important people in a Viking town were the chief and nobles (rich men). Next were traders, farmers and craft workers. At the bottom were slaves. The Vikings treated slaves very badly.

Noble   **Farmer**   **Slave**

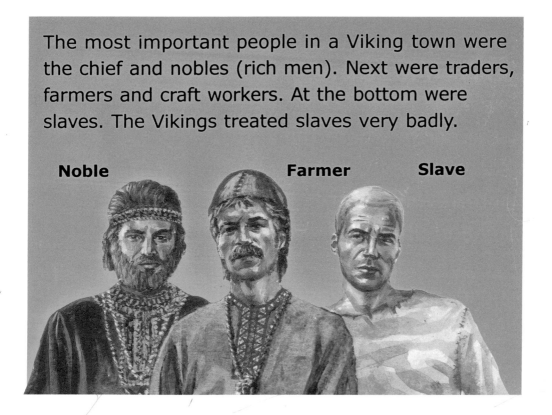

Some men fought each other to sort out an argument. The one with the worst wounds was the loser.

A Viking duel

Most of the time, the Vikings got on with each other. They learnt a set of rules, the *Hamaval*, which told them how to behave.

In the north, where the Vikings came from, the winter evenings are long and dreary.

To cheer themselves up, the Vikings held feasts in large, smoky halls.

After eating and drinking, they listened to long and exciting stories. Later, these stories, called "sagas", were written down. You can still read many of them today.

Some of the sagas were about real heroes like Harald Bluetooth and Erik the Red. They tell us a lot about the Vikings. Other stories were about the gods and their adventures.

A Viking feast

Odin, the god of war

Loki, the god of tricks

At first, the Vikings had many gods. They believed that each god had power over a part of their lives.

Odin was the one-eyed god of war. The Vikings believed he lived in a huge hall, called Valhalla. All warriors who died in battle went to live with Odin in Valhalla.

Thor

Dead Vikings were buried with their favourite things so they would have them in the next world.

Thor, the sky god, was famous for his mighty hammer.

The Vikings buried their chiefs in a ship, which they often set on fire. In Russia, Vikings killed a slave girl to go with the chief to the next world.

The Vikings were very fond of Thor and made magic charms in the shape of his hammer.

The Vikings who went south met the Christian religion. At first, they did not like it. It was not warlike enough for them.

A Viking cross

They destroyed many beautiful Christian churches. But Christian teachers gradually spread their religion among the Vikings.

The Vikings prayed to their gods in the open. They left food and drink for the gods to say thank you for their help.

A Viking church in Norway

The Vikings began to live more peaceful lives. Many of them married local people in Russia, Ireland, England and France.

Today, 900 years after the last Viking raids, it's hard to tell who is a Viking, and who isn't!

Find Out More

Many people living in Sweden, Norway and Denmark are proud of their Viking past. Lots of our words come from the Vikings too. Here are a few: law, leg, egg, freckle, skin and die. So every time you speak, read or write, remember these Viking words!

Days of the Week
Some days of the week are named after Viking gods. Thursday (Thor's day) is named after Thor.

The god Odin, also called Woden, gave us Wednesday (or Woden's day). Friday (or Frigga's day) is named after the Viking goddess Frigga.

UNUSUAL WORDS

Here we explain some words you may have read in this book.

Hamaval A set of rules that told Vikings how to live.
Knorr A Viking trading ship.
Longboat A Viking warship.
Northmen or Normans "People from the north" — another name for the Vikings.
Odin The Viking war god.

Saga A long story about the adventures of heroes and gods.
Thing The Viking word for a meeting or parliament.
Thor The Viking god of the sky.
Valhalla The hall where Odin lived.
Vineland or Vinland The place where the Vikings settled in North America.
Wattle and daub A way of making walls by covering woven sticks (wattle) with clay (daub).

The Oldest Parliament

Today, many countries decide new laws in meetings where everyone can speak. The Vikings held meetings like this. Their "Althing" in Iceland still meets today, 1,000 years later.

Up Hellya

The people of the Shetland Isles (see map on page 6) celebrate their Viking past. Every year they have a big feast called "Up Hellya". They burn a longboat and some of them dress up as Vikings.

Viking Towns

Many town names come from Viking words. The ending "-by" means farm. So the town of Appleby means "Apple-farm".

Who Came First?

Egyptians	Greeks	Romans	Vikings	Present Day
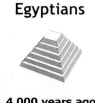				
4,000 years ago	2,500 years ago	2,000 years ago	1,000 years ago	Now

Index

ANSWERS TO PICTURE QUESTIONS

Page 16 In the Hedeby port scene, you can see blankets and shoes hanging from the shop and fruit on the donkey. A Viking is also repairing a cartwheel at the bottom of the picture.

Page 19 a is whale meat, **b** is a seagull, **c** is salmon (a large fish), **d** is seal, **e** is rabbit, **f** is polar bear.
Page 21 The woman is making clothes from leather. Did you see the sharp knife in her hand?

Illustrators: Steve Caldwell, Janie Pirie, Pete Roberts - Allied Artists; James Field, Stuart Lees, Ross Watton, Stephen Sweet - SGA; Ivan Lapper, Tony Smith, Peter Kesteven and Dave Burroughs. **Photocredits:** Abbreviations: t-top, m-middle, b-bottom. Cover - Photodisc; 3, 14, 21, 30, 31t, 31m, - Frank Spooner Pictures; 9, 29 - James Davis Travel Photography; 9 - Eye Ubiquitous; 22, 31b - Spectrum Color Library.